DEVOTIONAL
365 DAILY READINGS

PAHLINE HARDING

Copyright © 2012 Pahline Harding. All rights reserved. This book or any portion thereof may not be reproduced or used in any manner whatsoever without the express written permission of the publisher.

All scripture references taken from the New International Version. THE HOLY BIBLE< NIV ®, NIV ® Copyright © 1973, 1978, 1984, 2011 Biblica, Inc. Used by permission. All rights reserved worldwide.

January

1ˢᵗ January
Job

Relax more my child, don't get so tense and join in the dance sometimes. Invite heaven in and please don't stop praising me. I am always boasting about you! Remember Job? His sufferings did not last forever and neither will your troubles. I love you child, never forget that. My plans for you are for good, do not fear. I have your future secure in me.

2ⁿᵈ January
Ruth 2: 11-12

I have been made fully aware of how you have left your father, mother and the land of your birth and have come to a people unknown to you before. The Lord recompenses you for what you have done and a full reward will be given you, by the Lord the God of Israel, under whose wings you have come to trust.

3rd January
Psalm 3: 5-6
I lie down and sleep; I wake again, because the Lord sustains me.

Good morning Child.
This is a new day, a new start and a new opportunity. Lets walk through this day together, count on me; I will be there for you.

4th January
Mark 1: 35
Very early in the morning, while it was still dark, Jesus got up left the house and went off to a solitary place, where He prayed.

Good morning,
I'm so glad you made it! The farmers' best hours are in the early hours. He would miss the day if he got up late. Greet the dawn with me. I love you! The best is yet to come!

5th January
1 Corinthians 13:8
Love never fails

See through my eyes, see through the eyes of love, I see all things different to you, put on my glasses, love bears all things, love is a choice. Many choices. Choose love, be patient with yourself, I haven't finished with you yet. You are becoming the diamond you wanted to see in yourself. I see your struggles but keep going! I will not fail you!

6th January
Psalm 37: 4
Delight yourself in the Lord and He will give you the desires of your heart.

Our relationship can become ritualistic if its something you 'have to do', rather than want to or enjoy. Come on, enjoy me again; speak to me, sing to me, sit. Leave everything that burdens your mind and I will give you my peace. Go on your way rejoicing, easy isn't it!

7th January
Psalm 91: 1
He who dwells in the shelter of the Most High will rest in the shadow of the Almighty.

I wondered when you would find me. There is no other place to get peace than with me, why bother looking elsewhere? I am your peace, whatever the circumstances. I have much to share with you today. The rewards of spending time with me are manifold. I don't mind how you come, just come! Our times together are important for you, and are a joy to me.

8th January
Luke 5: 23
Which is easier to say? 'Your sins are forgiven,' or to say, 'Get up and walk'?

Rise up! Get going! Go forward, stop being double minded, your future awaits you! It is planned, you simply have to walk in it, knowing I have gone before you and will be with you! Time for action! Gird up the loins! Don't procrastinate. You are breaking through boundaries that were set against you and you will celebrate new beginnings with Me. Exciting days are ahead, you are stepping into destiny. Rise up, get going and find a sure path before you!

9th January
Joshua 3: 13
As soon as the priests who carry the ark of the Lord, the Lord of all the earth, set foot in the Jordan, its waters flowing downstream will be cut off and stand up in a heap.

Do not fear I am with you; take time to listen to me. It's time to move into what I have for you. Now is not the time to stand still. I am releasing you. I am wisdom, ask me and I will give it to you.

10th January
Nehemiah 4: 6
So we rebuilt the wall till all of it reached half its height, for the people worked with all their heart.

Do you know the key to success, building on what you have already started and just keep building! Do not give up, retreat or loose ground! Step by step, brick by brick, row on row, day by day, this is how you live, build and grow. Don't worry if things seem to be happening slowly, they will unfold and surprise you! The key to success is to keep building on what you have already accomplished and just keep building.

11th January
John 12: 24
I tell you the truth, unless a grain of wheat falls to the ground and dies, it remains only a single seed. But if it dies, it produces many seeds.

Ripples, ripples, ripples, no great work just ripples! One small stone can cause many ripples, affecting and influencing a great area. By throwing your life away, the ripples continue, they can cross- oceans, continents and countries. As you continue to throw your life away, so the ripples will continue to go out!

12th January
Hebrews 10: 38   Romans 1: 17
The Righteous will live by faith.

The just shall live by faith, faith in my love, my word, and my death. Without faith it is impossible to please me. Open wide the door of you heart, let me in to take over every area. Let me rule and reign, guide and lead. Trust me when I say I am faithful to fulfill all I have promised. Get excited for all I am planning for you.

13th January
Luke 24: 5
'Why do you look for the living among the dead?' He is not here He is risen!

I came to bring life. I came to break out of the shell of the expected. My life meant breaking out of the norm. It meant not settling for what was comfortable but being met by the unexpected. Is your life open-ended not neatly sewn up, leaving a lot of questions? Don't worry; breakthrough is nearer than you think.

14th January
Exodus 2: 3
When she could hide him no longer, she got a papyrus basket for him.

The seed has been sown, it's now time for the new shoots to start showing. There will be new growth this month. There will be more exposure in your life. The baby is getting to big to hide, it's time for the next step. The most unlikely people will be sent to help you. Don't worry if some things don't fit your expectations I can use anyone I want. Keep smiling it releases tension. I love you.

15th January
Exodus 3: 14
God said to Moses, 'I AM WHO I AM'.

Not was, not will be, I am. I am your covering, your delight, your source, your provision, your transport, your port, your destiny, your treasure, your rescue, your pleasure, your GOD, your desired haven, your finance, your love, your door, your vision, your dream, your power, your choice, your prophet, your father, your friend, your husband, your benefactor, your strength, your guide, your all.

16th January
Song of Solomon 2: 11
See! The winter is past; the rains are over and gone. Flowers appear on the earth.

Winter is over, spring has come, and new things are springing forth. You are dying to competition and insecurities and resting in my love. Even if I should elevate others above you, my love for you would not change. Love and pray for others as you would for yourself.

17th January
Genesis 12: 1
The Lord said to Abram, "Leave your country, your people and your father's household and go to the land I will show you."

Change can be painful when you have to leave behind people you love. The blessing of obedience comes at personal cost but releases enormous blessing for man

18th January
Revelation 3: 2
Wake up!

Wake up! Strengthen what remains and is about to die.
Wake up there is a world dying out there. They are not laughing. They are crying, hurting, bleeding. Only the truth of my gospel will set them free. Invest in eternal things, in lives. He who finds his life shall lose it and he who loses his life shall find it.

19th January
Jeremiah 31: 3
I have loved you with an everlasting love.

Sometimes we don't need to say anything clever or new, simply, ' I love you'. Are there any words more powerful or more sought after? Yes, I could say all kinds of clever things to you but 'I love you' will always be the most profound statement I could ever make.

20th January
Song of Solomon 4: 10
How much more pleasing is your love than wine.

Do you ever get bored with me? I never get bored with you. You are the apple of my eye, you bring me joy and excite me to passion. Every morning is a new expression of my love. You are special to me; a rose plucked, a firebrand spared, a jewel cast, my child.

21st January
Psalm 132: 18
His enemies will I clothe with shame, but upon himself shall his crown flourish.

Throw off gossip, negative talk and worry. Do not fret, but let me arise. I am with you, that is all you need. I am your biggest qualification, your most reliable source and your greatest ally. Rest assured we are in this together, whatever comes at you, comes at me, take heart I am there for you.

22nd January
I Corinthians 13
Now I will show you the most excellent way.

If love is the highest quality that man can attain to, why settle for less? Always strive for love. This is the mountain you are climbing, not one of selfish ambition but of loving to the uttermost. I am with you to live out this love and perfect love casts out fear. There is no need to fear, I love you.

23rd January
1 Corinthians 13: 12
Mirror image

When you look at yourself in the mirror, your mirror is out of focus and does not give a correct reflection. You see yourself as inadequate or unqualified. But the only true image is my word and what I say about you. This is the true and real self-image. You should see in my reflection that you are chosen, able, loved, productive, beautiful, fruitful, loving, destined, strong, set apart, sanctified and justified.

24th January
Revelation 3: 7
These are the words of Him who is holy and true, who holds the key of David.

Give me the keys to your life and let me be in control not you. You have a set of keys that keep you in control; give them to me. Let me open and close doors for you, for he who loses his life shall save it. Give me the reins of your life. I can only truly bless what has been entrusted to me.

25th January
Genesis 21: 1
The Lord did for Sarah what He had promised.

Do not despise those things that are birthed late in life. The dream inside you will bring you much joy. Remember, Sarah was old in years when she birthed the seed of a nation. Her joy was multiplied in later years. Don't despise starting things because you are older, if it is of God it can affect history! I will make you fruitful in old age.

26th January
This too shall pass.

27th January
Genesis 1: 31
God saw all that He had made and it was very good.

Good morning. It is good isn't it? Today is a good day because I made it. Enjoy today; ask me for big things not just small things. I would give you the nations if you asked me.

28th January
Proverbs 24: 16
Though a righteous man falls seven times, he rises again.

Its not how many times you fall that counts its how many times you get up. I love you; fight one more round.

29th January
James 2: 23
He was called God's friend.

I call you friend.

30th January
Romans 6: 11

Count yourself dead to sin.

Reckon yourself dead to sin and alive to Christ. It's true, I do not want my children in condemnation I want them free by appropriating my cross. I took all your sins upon the cross so you could be free; sin does not have to be a part of you.

31st January
Matthew 28: 19

GO!

February

1st February
John 15: 7
If you remain in me and my word remains in you, ask whatever you wish, and it will be given you.

Go on ask!

2nd February
Matthew 6:25
Do not worry about your life.

My child, do not worry about anything; I am with you. Keep our relationship simple. Even a child can understand my ways. Trust me I know what I am doing. Live each day in obedience to my will and I will make the way clear, the mist will lift and you will see what you should be doing.

3rd February
Revelation 3:19
Be earnest and repent.

I am calling my people to repentance because I want to pour out my Spirit upon them again. Listen to me and live. Yes, listen and obey my words and you shall live, you shall not die. Turn around; change the way you are living. Sorrow for sin is not enough in itself; you must turn around and go in the opposite direction.

4th February
Genesis 19:17
Don't look back and don't stop anywhere.

Keep going; do not look back. As I rescued Lot, so I will rescue you. Don't look back, turn your back on sin and keep walking. I am with you; you cannot fail. Keep looking to me. I can rescue you from the sin that knocks at the door of your life. Submit to me, trust me and live. Walk with me today; I am not a God of depression but a God of joy.

5th February
Luke15: 20
While he was still a long way off, his father saw him and was filled with compassion.

Welcome back, you made it. Did you think I would abandon you because you moved out of my will? It is always my will to care for my children. I have seen your struggles and my plans for you are still working for your good.

6th February
I Kings 17:13
First make a small cake of bread for me.

Do not choose when you think it will be a good time to give. Is there someone in need in your life now? Elijah's widow gave the little she had and God multiplied it. It is not what a man has that makes him great but how much he gives away.

7th February
Isaiah 52:1
Awake, awake, O Zion.

Wake up! I am calling you. I am waking you in the mornings to be with me. Get up do not stay in bed. Too much bed equals dead spiritually.

8th February
Psalm 2:8

What do you want me to do for you? Ask ME, and I will give you the nations. I love and cherish you. Keep walking in my will for I have great plans for you.

9th February
Matthew 14:29
'Come' He said.

Walk the storm with me; you will not be overwhelmed. I am with you, trust me, I know your struggles, your dreams, your hopes; they are wrapped up in me. Shake off those things that would attack your body and live. You are a microcosm of my world and my world is life.

10th February
Luke 22:26
The greatest among you should be like the youngest.

Die to self and live to all I have for you. Don't strive for position or a name; I will give it to you. Come back to me that is all you need.

11th February
Matthew 26:10
She has done a beautiful thing to me.

People see time and gifts spent on me as wasted. But I receive such offerings as love being poured out. The woman who anointed my feet did not know another way to express her love towards me. By this act she was saying that I was worth the most expensive thing she had. What is the most expensive thing you possess, is it your time, reputation, praise? Would you be willing to waste it on me?

12th February
Psalm 34:19
A righteous man may have many troubles, but the Lord delivers him from them all.

Do not fear the evil one. I led captivity captive. I overcame the world and death. Do not fear; many are the afflictions of the righteous but I deliver them out of them all. Keep going with all I put in your heart. Study the word and let my word enrich and feed you. Then I can use you to feed others. Start today.

13th February
Psalm 19:1
The heavens declare the glory of God.

Look up, the Heavens declare the power of God and they were established by my hand. Take my hand and I'll lead you. Don't stay where you are; move on. Time to expand, time to increase. I know that you are pregnant with my vision and I am watching over my word to perform it.

14th February
Jeremiah 29:11
'For I know the plans I have for you', declares the Lord, 'plans to prosper you'.

Calm down. Getting in a fuss will not produce the works of God or move me to act any quicker. I have already said there is a move taking place. Therefore, hold on to my word and keep in peace, as I work out my purposes for you. You want to be released from your containment so you shall be. Meanwhile, please don't make life unpleasant for those around you.

15th February
Revelation 3:8
See, I have placed before you an open door.

I know you are not seeing clearly at the moment; but you will. The way will be made clear, don't fret, be still and know that I am God. There is a way out. It is not always obvious. Sometimes doors do not look like doors, but they are. Push and one might just open.

16th February
I Corinthians 16:9
A great door for effective work has opened for me.

It will not be long now, so be prepared. If I close one door I open another. This time has been necessary for you. Come on take my hand. Stop fearing man and break free in my Spirit.

17th February
Matthew 14:31
Immediately Jesus reached out His hand and caught him.

I am reaching down, ready to lift you up. Take my hand, you will not drown, you will not be overcome I am coming to save you. You think you have to fight this battle and that you have to work it out. Do not worry, I am coming to save you. The very waves sent to take you down will lift you up. I love you, I always have.

18th February
John 19:30
It is finished!

The battle is over. The war that has been going on around you is over.

19th February
Psalm 73:26
My flesh and my heart may fail, but God is the strength of my heart.

Do not resist change; keep flexible. I use change to bring about my purposes. Move with me and not against me.

20th February
Hebrews 13: 8
Jesus Christ the same yesterday, today and forever.

I am here. I am the same yesterday, today and forever. I do not change. I am no respecter of persons. What I have done for one I will do for another. Trust me, your faith changes, my love doesn't. Think big, act big, as if you worship a big God. I will not fail you.

21st February
Exodus 13: 14
I AM WHO I AM

Remember, I am with you, the great I AM. Whatever I give you, give out; don't hold back, you will not be contained. Your passion will ignite others and they will be drawn to me. Come on follow me, we have new places to go and people to meet, I will make you a fisher of men. I have cut the cords that held you back; the traditions and fear of man, you are free to go forward and seize the opportunities that will come to you.

22nd February
James 1:5
If any of you lacks wisdom, he should ask God

I see you need help with this new relationship. Ask me and I will give you my wisdom.
My wisdom will fill your thoughts, words and actions, causing you to be able to see clearly and act righteously. Go slower and you will hear clearer.

23rd February
Isaiah 51: 3
He will make her deserts like Eden.

The more you submit to me, the more I will raise you up. I hear every cry; I catch every tear. Though your life has been like a wasteland it will become as the Garden of Eden. We are not finished yet. There is a door open to an enlarged place and the key of submission has opened it for you.

24th February
Judges 4: 4
Deborah, a prophetess, was leading Israel at that time.

I am about to birth something new. I am birthing a generation of women old and young who will dare to believe my word and shake this world with it. Watch and see what I am about to do. A new army of women is emerging with the Deborah spirit and who carry the heart of Mary.

25th February
Proverbs 31:15
She gets up while it is still dark.

She does not simply wake; she gets up!
Get yourself out of bed. It is essential to rise early and to be prepared for the day in me.

26th February
Proverbs 29: 1
A man who remains stiff necked after many rebukes will suddenly be destroyed- without remedy.

Do not keep resisting the work of My Spirit I want to bless you not destroy you.

27th February
Psalm 91. Psalm 37

Fear not! Fear no man! Though an army comes against you; you are safe in me.

28th February
Joshua 14: 12
Give me this mountain!

Keep climbing; keep pressing forward. Do not turn back! Mediocrity is settling half way up the mountain. Do not settle! Go all the way and take your mountain.

March

1st March
Luke 6: 48
When the flood came, the torrent struck that house but could not shake it.

Rest in me, it does not help when your emotions are in turbulence. Seek the quiet place in the eye of storm. Storms and waves will hit in you life, it is learning to deal with them in me that is important. Do not let your emotions be in control, you must learn to rule over your emotions.

2nd March
Romans 5: 5
Hope does not disappoint us.

Do not give up, the turning point is just around the corner. Keep going. I will not disappoint you.

3rd March
John 15: 16
I chose you and appointed you to go and bear fruit.

Push through to be all you can be.
I love you, I cherish you and I see all you are becoming. I see your desires being fulfilled. Live your dreams now, don't waste another day. Write, dream, speak, or dance, whatever you want to do; do it now! These are your days use them, do not abuse them or neglect them.

4th March
2 Corinthians 12: 8
My grace is sufficient for you.

Keep seeking me do not give in to feelings. Obedience can be carried out without feelings. I will bless your efforts with success. Trust me I will go with you. Do not forsake our times together. I will open doors to unexpected places as you seek my Glory.
I am with you that is all you need. My power shows up best in weak people.

5th March
Proverbs 22: 29
See a man skilled in his work; he will serve before Kings; he will not serve before obscure men.

Whatever you do – do it with all your might as unto the Lord.

6th March
Proverbs 12:24
The hand of the diligent shall rule

Work, for I am with you. I will bless the work of your hands. Use your time wisely. Accept each day as a gift from me and use it wisely. I give each day as a gift to you. I do not manipulate or control, I simply ask if you will be willing to obey the promptings of my Spirit. When I ask do not delay but act immediately.

7th March
Isaiah 54:15
If anyone does attack you it will not be my doing.

Trust me. Come with me to the high places where you will be kept safe under the shadow of my wings. I am with you and will not fail you. I will be with you in trouble and the floods will not overwhelm you. I love you, whoever touches you sticks his finger in my eye. Every tongue that rises against you in judgment you shall condemn and show to be in the wrong.

8th March
Psalm 42 & 43
Why so cast down O my soul? Trust in God for you shall yet Praise Him your Saviour and your God.

9th March
Nehemiah 4: 9
They tried to frighten us but I prayed, 'Now strengthen my hands'.

Opposition often comes in the form of intimidation to try to get you to retreat or step out of your call. The enemy will accuse you of all sorts of things and try to make you feel inadequate for the task. But God has called you, commissioned you and He will keep you. Do not back down but ask God to strengthen you to keep going.

10th March
Isaiah 43: 18
Forget the former things; do not dwell on the past.

Do not look to the old ways you have done things; it is a new day. There is a fresh wind blowing through the church bringing new things with it. The old is being challenged and the new will shake those things not rooted in me. Be ready in this new move to move with me. I am demolishing the old structures that were born out of traditionalism and religion in the church and building My Kingdom.

11th March
Matthew 26: 39
My Father, not as I will, but as you will.

I am waiting for you to give up the struggle to do my will and say, 'Yes' to me. Say, 'Yes', to My Spirit and give up the rights to yourself. Say, 'Yes' to obedience to me and no to self. Obedience to my will brings power.

12th March
Genesis 12: 2
I will bless you

I am the God of Abraham, Isaac and Jacob. The God who walked with Abraham, is the same God that meets with you now. I reward faith and bless those who trust me. Think of the faith of Abraham. I want you to inherit all I have for you. Don't lose your inheritance, hold on expectantly and your faith will be rewarded.

13th March
John 21: 17
Feed my sheep.

Take what I give you and give it to my sheep. Beware of selfish ambition, keep serving me and live for others.

14th March
Psalm 30: 5
Weeping may remain for a night, but rejoicing comes in the morning.

All my promises are yes and amen in Christ Jesus. What I promise is as good as done. The cross of Jesus redeemed the pain sin had caused. The cross will also redeem your situation. You may be weeping now but there will be joy again.

15th March
II Tim 2: 3
Endure hardness like a good soldier of Christ Jesus.

I am fitting you for service; like a soldier, I am preparing you for action. I am waiting to bring about your hearts desires but you must be willing to pay the cost of your dream; which is faithfulness, self-denial and diligence. Those whose dreams have come true have disciplined their lives. It is those who have enlisted who are under authority; I do not command civilians.

16th March
John 14: 6
Jesus answered, 'I am the way the truth and the life.'

Do not fear the days ahead I have gone before you. I have gone ahead of you and I am big enough to handle every situation that arises in your life. Keep the joy, keep the dance and don't lose sight of me. If a door closes, trust me, you didn't need what was beyond it. The doors I open will excite you and lead you into what you desire.

17th March
John 7: 37
Let him come to me and drink.

Come to the waters and drink. Take as much or as little as you desire. Remember, when the Israelites were in the desert they collected the manna. Some of them collected little, some collected much; but none lacked. I satisfy the longing soul with good things. Come drink of me and never thirst again.

18th March
Romans 12: 2
Be not conformed to this world but be transformed by the renewing of your mind.

Your mind will be transformed as you live in the word of My Spirit. It will be a living agent at work in you, changing and renewing the way you think. Your mind has been programmed a certain way for years. My word will undo that which was false and release you into the living truth of my word.

19th March
Genesis 15: 6
Abram believed the Lord.

You are finally beginning to believe that I have good plans for your life. Abraham and Sarah experienced life like you; family feuds, tensions, jealousies, mistakes. As they waited for my promises to unfold, they eat, got up, worked and walked with me. Trust me that the bigger picture for your family is greater than you could ever imagine.

20th March
Psalm 91: 4
Under His wings you will find refuge.

Don't Worry! Worry is a sin. Hand everything over to me and watch me take care of the issues that wear you down. It is a choice, worrying is a choice. Either you give your burdens to me or you keep them. Cast your burdens on the Lord and He will sustain you. I don't want you to worry about anything today. I want you to be as free as a child secure in his Father's love.

21st March
Deut 6: 5
Love the Lord your God with all your heart and soul and strength.

Have you forgotten the Golden Rule so soon? To love me with all your heart, soul and strength, and your neighbor as yourself. Is that so hard? Thinking of others flows out of communion with me.

22nd March
Hebrews 13: 5
Never will I fail you never will I forsake you.

Thinking of giving up? You have come to the right place. I am your energy restorer, hope giver, dream maker. I am everything you need. You are nearer reaching your dream than you know. Do not give up. The darkest hour is just before dawn.

23rd March
Psalm 108: 2
I will awaken the dawn.

How about waking the dawn together and spending some secret moments in the womb of the day. I'll be waiting. It's an amazing time. Creation waits for the dawn like the audience waits for the curtain to lift. Anticipation, expectation, there is no other time like it in the day. Come into the secret place with me, reserved for you.

24th March
Exodus

It's time to pick up. There is a time for laying down and a time for picking up. This is the season for picking up those talents, friends, dreams and gifts I have given you and use them for my purpose. What is in your hand will you use it for me? Do not despise the things that look small in the eyes of man. I can use a cruise of oil, a pebble or two small fish and five small loaves.

25th March
Job 23: 10
When he has tested me, I shall come forth as gold.

The goldsmith or silversmith takes his piece of metal and dips it in the furnace and then forms the gold into something precious. He takes much care not to destroy it in the process. I have tested, tried and forged you to make you into the person you are today. You have been in and out of the furnace and I am about to fill you with my Glory.

26th March
Exodus 14:21
The waters were divided and the Israelites went through on dry ground.

Remember, when I parted the Red Sea for Moses and the children of Israel. All I had to do was breathe and the waters resided. I have parted the waters once and I can do it again. If you ask me I will part the waters for you, your gifting and your ministry. All you have to do is believe and you will see miracles. Could it be you I use to demonstrate my love and power?

27th March
Hebrews 12: 1-2
Run with perseverance keeping your eyes on Jesus.

I will deliver you from your fears, no turning back, no double-mindedness. Keep your eye focused on the goal. You have said yes to me, will you now back down at the first sign of adversity? Come on, keep running, nothing shall hold you back. You shall overcome every hurdle in your way. Run to win.

28th March
Exodus 3: 10
Now go, I am sending you.

Are you excited? You should be. I am answering your prayers and you will see a turnaround in your situation. There is a world to be won and so few willing to go for me. If you will go then I will use you, your voice and your personality to bring lost souls to me. But I need your permission.

29th March
James 4: 10
Humble yourselves before the Lord, and he will lift you up.

Promotion always follows a time of humility and repentance. Get ready to be lifted up to new heights for I have seen the contrition of your heart as you have humbled yourself before me.

30th March
Psalm 51: 11
Cast me not away from your presence.

I have not cast you off, far from it. I am waiting for you to line up with me and obey me. I have forgiven you so what are you waiting for? I can do all things so expect great things this year and you will see them. Prepare your heart for all I have for you.

31st March
Philippians 4: 6
Do not be anxious about anything, but with thanksgiving, present your requests to God.

A thank you would be appreciated now and again. I am excited because this day is special. It is the only one of it's kind and I am going to enjoy it. Look around for the special little things that will brighten your day, birds, animals and children. Or look for ways you can praise others. Go on bless someone today and you will feel much better.

April

1st April
Psalm 46: 10
Be still, and know that I am God.

Why do you fear man and do not fear me the God of the universe. Why do you fear man's voice and not my voice on judgment day? Am I such a weak God to you? Be at peace, be still and know that I am God.

2nd April
James 4: 7
Resist the devil and he will flee from you.

Confront child and do not be afraid. Be on the offensive against the enemy. Yes, run to the battle.

3rd April
Nehemiah 4: 6

I know that you have met resistance as you have sought to spend time with me, but don't worry. The resistance is breaking and you will soon move into a larger place. You will spend more time with me this year and people will be drawn to your flame as you catch the fire from me. You will be as a living torch, which will set others alight. They will not necessarily approve of you, but do not look for man's approval. I approve of you

4th April
Ecclesiastes 11: 1
Cast your bread upon the waters for after many days you will find it.

Give away; do not hold on to possessions, finances, gifts etc. Release them to others and they will return to you in due season.

5th April
Psalm 119: 67
Before I was afflicted I went astray, but now I obey your word.

Love without discipline does not produce good fruit. God disciplines because He loves us. Pain can be the most effective agent for change if we allow God to use the pain in our lives for good.

6th April
Isaiah 58: 14
I will cause you to ride on the heights of the land.

Aspire to new heights. Come into a new order in your life that will enable you to rise above your circumstances and other limitations. Soar to new heights in My Spirit. Leave the old ways behind and come into the true fast.

7th April
Ephesians 6: 13
After you have done everything, stand.

Stay where you are, don't move. Remember, if you cannot go forward, stand your ground and do not retreat. Do not give into the pressure to back off or back down. There is a way out and I will show you. Look at me, do not compromise but keep going forward. I Love you.

8th April
John 7: 37
If anyone is thirsty, let him come to me and drink.

Just as the body needs water to maintain it, so you need the water of My Spirit to refresh and renew you. You need my anointing for all you want to do. Come back and return to me, the fountainhead. You want a holiday, just ask me and I'll show you where to go. I will bless you.

9th April
Matthew 6: 16
When you fast, your father will reward you.

Need help in your prayers try fasting!

10th April
John 11: 25
I am the resurrection and the life.

You are on the right track keep going. Did I not tell you that if you believed you would see my Glory. Believe me for miracles, transformation and healing. No matter how dead your situation looks, I am the resurrection and the life.

11th April
Ecclesiastes 7: 9
Do not be quick to be angry.

Have you allowed yourself to sin by getting angry? Turn back to God and allow Him to cleanse and touch your mouth with the burning coals of His forgiveness.
Renounce any unrighteous anger and be filled again with the Holy Spirit.

12th April
Philippians 2: 9
God gave Him the name that is above every name.

I can't help smiling at what I have in store for you. Man's rejection brings my promotion. After Jesus was rejected and crucified He was exalted to the highest honor and given a name above all names.

13th April
1 Corinthians 6: 19
Do you not know that your body is a temple of the Holy Spirit?

Your body is the temple of the Holy Spirit and I want you to treat it respectfully. Eat nothing that would dishonor this temple. Be disciplined in all you do this year. For whatever you do; whether you eat or drink do all to the Glory of God.

14th April
Isaiah 52: 1
Awake, awake, clothe yourself with strength.

Wake up, this is definitely not the time to sleep! There is much to be done. Pray for My will to be done and trust me. This year will be a year of hard work but the sowing will reap great reward and harvest. Don't delay start today.

15th April
Isaiah 60:1
Arise, shine for your light has come.

Now is the time to awake out of your complacency and slumber. Arise, and proclaim my word. Arise and set the captives free with my word. Arise and establish my works on the earth. I am calling you to lead my people and to shine for me in the darkness. Keep our times together as priority. Do not leave the altar of God. My plans for you are great.

16th April
Luke 15: 22
Put a ring on his finger.

Stretch out your hand. I have placed my ring on your finger and given you my authority. Walk and rule as a child who has my authority.

17th April
John 16: 24
Ask and you will receive, that your joy may be full.

Expect the unexpected. Expect to be surprised by my presence. I have so much to give and so few who will receive what I have. Take all you want, just ask. Open up my storehouse that others may go in and receive.

18th April
Joshua 1: 5
No one will be able to stand against you all the days of your life.

You are entering a land occupied by an enemy. But take heart, you are well equipped to take the land and conquer it. I have given you power over all the power of the enemy and nothing shall by any means harm you. I am with you always. Fear not, greater is He within you than He that is against you. I am opening up the way for you to take cities in my name.

19th April
Luke 6: 38
Give and it will be given to you.

I am counting; counting how much has been given for my kingdom. I am waiting to pour out of the Heavenly bank account and bless you, but there is only little coming in. I am not storing up in Heaven for me; I am storing up for you. Give and it shall be given back to you pressed down, shaken together and running over.

20th April
Psalm 86:17
Give me a sign of your goodness that my enemies may see it and be put to shame.
For you, O Lord, have helped me and comforted me.

Please give me a sign Lord!

21st April
John 14: 14
You may ask me for anything in my name and I will do it.

Think big. As you seek me you shall find all. Trust Me; I am leading you. I hear the unspoken whispers of your heart and am ever planning for you in love. Plan for something you cannot do in yourself.

22nd April
Genesis 21: 1
The Lord visited Sarah as He had said.

Anointed one, my anointing comes with responsibility. Is anything too hard or too wonderful for the Lord? At the appointed time Sarah gave birth to the promise and so shall you.

23rd April
John 14: 12
He will do even greater things than these.

Remember all I achieved in three years. I poured out in three years all that had been invested in me. Read the Gospels again and do all you see and hear. Do not despise these days. Live for today.

24th April
Philippians 3:14
I press on!

It is not too late. There is still much to do. Move on; don't stand looking back. Leave the regrets for there is nothing you can do to change the past. However, you can change the future. Start now with what you have. Be faithful with what you have now.

25th April
Genesis 21: 14
Abraham rose the next morning.

Don't delay, do it now or you may lose the opportunity. Write that book, make that phone call, pray that prayer. Delayed obedience is disobedience. Why are you waiting? Life is going on. Abraham got up the very next morning in obedience to my call. Ezekiel ministered the day he lost his wife. Come on do something, do not just sit there.

26th April
Matthew 7: 7
Knock and the door shall be opened.

Keep trying the doors; do not give up. Doors are opening in your life, now. I have always led you and will now. Your destiny will open up keep knocking on the doors.

27th April
Exodus 14: 14
The Lord will fight for you.

Take heart child, the Lord is coming to save you. He will fight for you. Angels are being released to strengthen you. The enemies you face today you will not see tomorrow. Trust Me in this.

28th April
Psalm 37: 1
Do not fret because of evil men.

Why do you fret? Your heavenly father is with you and will keep you. I will not fail you or forsake you. You are in the palm of my hand. Trust me to guard all that you entrust to me. I will not leave you as an orphan but I will bless you and give you success. Step out, knowing I AM.

29th April
Jeremiah 29:14
I will be found by you.

Do not miss what God has for you. Now is the time, what are you waiting for? Ask me and I will show you things you know not. Breakout, there is no one holding you back but you. Take hold of those things you have dreamt of. Do not hold back because of the cost.

30th April
Psalm 32: 8
I will instruct you and teach you in the way you should go.

You are at the crossroads. I am going to show you the way. I will instruct you and guide you with my eye. Just allow me to lead you; I am in the car with you and I hold the map to your destiny.

May

1st May
Ecclesiastes 7: 8
The end of a matter is better than it's beginning.

Finish what you have started. The end of a thing is better than the beginning. You run well, what has hindered you? Keep going and keep pressing forward. Do not hold back. Give everything you have to obtain the prize. It's not how you start but how you finish that is important.

2nd May
Psalm 62: 8
Pour out your heart to Him.

What is in your heart? Pour out your heart before me; I am a refuge for you. Trust Me I know what I am doing. All will become clear. Keep praising me and do what I have already given you to do.

3rd May
Ecclesiastes 3:4
There is a time to mourn and a time to dance.

Your days of mourning are ended; it's time to put on your dancing shoes.

4th May
Song of Solomon 8: 5
Under the apple tree I roused you.

Come and sit under my shade; let us eat the apples of love and spend time together. Come and get refreshed in my presence. I know everyone demands on you but I desire your company. Come let us eat together, just to be together. I don't want to use and abuse you. I simple want to love you.

5th May
Genesis 26: 12
Isaac planted crops in that land and the same year reaped a hundredfold, because the Lord blessed him.

Trust Me, I know what I am doing. This year will be a time of sowing and reaping. Begin to live again and expect great things. You think to small. Think, plan, work and I will give you success. What do you want to see in the year ahead? Adjust your thinking and do not limit me.

6th May
Jeremiah 18: 6
Like clay in the hand of the potter.

I am chipping away at you, like a sculptor with his masterpiece. I am making you more like me. I am the potter and you are the clay. You are gradually becoming the likeness of me. Thank you for taking time to be with me. I love you. Many are called but few are chosen.

7th May
Joshua 3:4
You have never been this way before.

I am calling you this day to make a difference, to blaze a way for others to follow. I am not deliberately hiding my way from you but I need you to search for my purpose. The searching will make you stronger and clearer.

8th May
Jonah 2. 2-3
Your waves and breakers swept over me.

I have let you go into the depths and you have cried out to me from the depths. I will deliver you. You will come out with a new song. In the depths you learn a new song of thanksgiving and praise to me. Like Jonah, you will come out of the depths with new power. You cannot escape My Presence. Even if you go down to the depths, behold I am there.

9th May
Psalm 139: 14
I am fearfully and wonderfully made.

Struggling child, you have looked at others and thought you should do better. Really child, do you think I hold my children up in comparison to one another? No, child the only comparison I make is with my son Jesus and you match perfectly. All I see in you is Him. Have you forgotten the Cross? I've done it all for you. No more sweat child, simply rest in what I have already done.

10th May
John 7: 37
Streams of living water will flow from within him.

Be strong in your inner man. I am with you. My name will be glorified through you. Rivers of living water will flow through you. Your scars will no longer hurt you. I will heal them. I will give streams in the desert; the Glory of the Lord will rest upon you.

11th May
Hebrews 10: 35-36
You need to persevere so that when you have done the will of God, you will receive what He has Promised.

You are not the only one who thinks I am moving 'too slow'.

12th May
1 Samuel 15:22
To obey is better than sacrifice.

It is easier to ask me for a new word than to obey what I have already said. Take time today to review what I have already asked of you and just 'do it'. Then further revelation will come to you.

13th May
Isaiah 40: 31
Those who hope in the Lord will renew their strength.

As your days so shall your strength be. I give power to the tired and worn out and strength to the weak. My power shows up best in weak people. I am with you that is all you need. Rise up afresh with strength.

14th May
Ruth 2: 3
So she went out and began to glean in the fields.

The harvest is there for you but it will not come to you, you must go to get it. I will give you the field as I gave to Ruth, you will not always be gleaning the edges.

15th May

Micah 2: 13
Their King will pass through before them.

I am making a way, I am making a way; I am making a way. Do not fear what will happen to you. I am the breaker-Messiah and I will break open the way for you. I am the Lord who opened the way in for you in the past and I will break open the way for you again. You are not trapped; I am in control. Do not be cowardly but courageous. I will make a way for you.

16th May
Psalm 42-43
Why are you downcast, o my soul?

The very thing that is weighing you down today, you will yet praise me for. The very thing that upsets you today, you will laugh about in the future.

17th May
Hosea 2: 15
I will make the valley of Achor (trouble) a door of hope.

I work all things together for good as you continue to love and seek me.

18th May
Proverbs 3: 6
In all your ways acknowledge Him and He will make your paths straight.

Never make decisions without prayer!

19th May
1 Samuel 15: 23
Rebellion is like the sin of divination, and stubbornness like the evil of idolatry.

Please stop resisting me and submit to my will and you will have peace.

20th May
Matthew 14: 29
Then Peter got out of the boat, walked on the water and came towards Jesus.

Now is not the time to run back to the safety of the shore. As you venture out of your comfort zone you will find me there. I rule over the seas and storms and nothing can stop you. I am looking for those bold enough to step out and trust me.

21st May
Isaiah 49: 2
In the shadow of his hand he hid me.

You are not forgotten, I am preparing you and polishing you as my arrow. When I release you, you will hit the mark for which I made you. Do not despise the days in my quiver for they are preparing you to fly.

22nd May
2 Peter 3: 10
The day of the Lord will come like a thief.

Countdown has begun; these days are numbered. Live each moment for my purposes. I am coming back soon. Make each day count.

23rd May
I Corinthians 4: 20
The Kingdom of God is not a matter of talk but of power.

Less talk and more reliance on My Holy Spirit will bring about my Kingdom in your life.

24th May
2 Corinthians 1: 8
We were under great pressure, far beyond our ability to endure, so that we despaired even of life. But this happened that we might not rely on ourselves but on God, who raises the dead.

The fiery trials you are going through are to help you depend more on me. As you place the whole weight of your circumstances on me I will lift you up on Eagle's wings.

25th May
2 Corinthians 4: 7
We have this treasure in jars of clay to show that this all-surpassing power is from God and not from us.

I understand your weaknesses and allow you the privilege of being a weak vessel so that nobody is confused where the Glory in you comes from.

26th May
Isaiah 40: 27
Hope (wait) in the Lord.

What does wait on the Lord mean? It means 'wait' on the Lord. Do not act before you have spent time with the Holy Spirit.

27th May
Deut 17: 16
You are not to go back that way again.

You have left the past, now keep going forward. You cannot return. It will grieve me if you even look back.

28th May
Colossians 3: 13
Forgive as the Lord forgave you.

True forgiveness will always see the other person as though they had never caused the offense in the first place.

29th May
Matthew 5: 44
Love your enemies.

Love your enemies, do good to them, if they are hungry, feed them. Act nobly to those who hate you, do not say you will pay him back. Invoke blessings upon and pray for the happiness of those who curse you. This will make you like me.

30th May
Psalm 105: 18
His neck was put in irons.

I am putting iron into your soul and making you strong to overcome your adversaries. You will not keep tripping over the snares laid for you by the enemy. But you will overcome as you obey and keep close to me. I will make your face as flint and you will be feared. You will stand your ground and the enemy will flee from you.

31st May
2 Timothy 1: 7
For I have given you a spirit of power, of love and of self-discipline.

I have delivered you from a spirit of cowardice and I am making you fearless and bold. When people look at you they will not see timidity but boldness and courage.

June

1st June
Exodus 4: 2
What is that in your hand?

What is that you have in your hand? You have in your hand a seed. You hold a seed of money, a gift, a talent or a dream. Be willing to give it to me and I will anoint it, use it and multiply it.

2nd June
Genesis 12: 3
Whoever curses you I will curse.

I want you to be free from the fear of man and being a people pleaser. All you need is status with me, not the praise of man.
For the applause of Heaven you must forego the praise of man.

3rd June
Genesis 21: 14
The next morning!

Instant obedience is the only form of obedience. Delayed obedience is disobedience. I have asked you to step out in faith, do not put off my call, just do it.

4th June
Isaiah 33: 21
There the Lord will be our Mighty One.

You are wondering what is holding up the answer to your prayer. I am the place of broad rivers and streams. Trust me, this containment will open up to a spacious place for you. Maybe you are hoping for too little when I want to give much more than you are asking for.

5th June
Ephesians 6: 12
Our struggle is not against flesh and blood.

Remember who you are child and whose authority you carry. Nothing shall by any means hurt you as you walk in the authority I have given you. Your fight is not against flesh and blood but the principalities and powers of this world. You are of another Kingdom and you rule over this earth.

6th June
Psalm 2: 8
Ask me and I will give you the nations.

7th June
Psalm 37: 7-11
Do not fret when men succeed in their ways.

Do not fret at those who are coming against you. You will look around and they will be gone. Be patient, trust me and I will act for you.

8th June
Psalm 23: 4
Though I walk through the valley of the shadow of death, I will fear no evil.

When you walk through the shadow of death I will be with you. I will uphold you in your grief and confusion and will carry you through to other side of the valley.

9th June
Haggai 2: 18
From this day on I will bless you.

The glory of your latter years will be greater than the former and I will give you peace.

10th June
Luke 9: 62
No one who puts his hand to the plough and looks back is fit for service in the kingdom of God.

Do not keep looking over your shoulder but move on in what I have for you. Walk in the new thing I am doing. Keep going forward.

11th June
Psalm 40: 2
He lifted me out of the slimy pit.

As you wait on me I will lift you out of despair, make you secure, position you for blessing and put a new song in your mouth.

12th June
John 15: 1-2
My Father is the Gardener.

Be encouraged if you are being pruned back. I only prune the branches where I see life and expectancy. I cut off the dead branches!

13th June
John 15: 4
Neither can you bear fruit unless you remain in me.

I know the frustration you have of wanting to work independent of me. But without me you will accomplish no lasting fruit. You may be busy, but where is the fruit?

14th June
Isaiah 32: 9-13
In little more than a year you who feel secure will tremble.

Beware of complacency! What do you expect to see in one year? If you want change, if you want a harvest of good fruit in your relationships, finances, church, then sow. Sow your seeds today for a better tomorrow. Don't put it off.

15th June
Luke 13: 8
Leave it alone for one more year.

I will be looking for the fruit of our relationship in a year's time and what will I find?
Let this be a year of increase for my kingdom in your life. I will be back.

16th June
Hebrews 6: 7
God is not unjust; He will not forget your work.

If I have blessed you then go out and bless someone else. I expect to see fruit spring up from the blessings I pour upon you.

17th June
Joshua 3:16
So the people crossed over opposite Jericho.

No retreat- keep advancing. Whatever your Jordan is, do not be dismayed, keep on doing what I have given you to do. Provision and breakthrough are coming your way, simply refuse to retreat.

18th June
Ecclesiastes 7: 8
For the end of a matter is better than it's beginning.

Keep on building. If the desire is to quit and give up half way through a task then ask me for a spirit of finishing. There will be a harvest of blessing if you do not get discouraged and give up.

19th June
Galatians 6: 9
Let us not become weary in doing good.

I know you are tired and you wonder if I am really going to bring about all I have promised. But you know that nothing you do for me is ever wasted. There will be a harvest of blessing if you don't get discouraged and give up.

20th June
Romans 12: 11
Never be lacking in zeal, but keep your spiritual fervour.

Do not allow laziness to be an excuse to disobey the Lord. Remember the story of the talents. The servant told the owner that he was afraid to use the talents. But the owner accused him instead of being lazy. Do not use fear as an excuse for laziness.

21st June
Ecclesiastes 9:10
Whatever your hand finds to do, do it with all your might.

Whatever you do for me, do well. If you run the teas and coffees at church; work in the crèche or give lifts, remember you are doing it as unto me. To work well and cheerfully honors me and brings great reward.

22nd June
Matthew 26:48 27:31
The one I kiss is the man.
They led Him away to crucify Him.

The little things in life are important and can be powerful. A smile, a kiss, a hug, can brighten someone's day. The little things make or break our day. A kiss and three nails, so insignificant yet so powerful.

23rd June
Matthew 26:48 27:31
The one I kiss is the man.

Betrayed by a kiss. If you have known the kiss of betrayal, you have come near the cross. Give the hurt of betrayal to me. I have taken the pain of betrayal at Calvary so that you will not have to carry it. The answer to the pain of betrayal is simple; forgive!

24th June
Psalm 41: 9
Even my close friend, whom I trusted, has lifted up his heel against me.

If you know the pain of being let down or hurt by someone close to you; let me into your pain. I was anointed to heal the broken hearted and bind up their wounds.

25th June

I Love You, I Love You, I Love You.

26th June
Isaiah 54 1-3
Enlarge the place of your tent.

The place you are in has become too small. I will bring you into new partnerships, new relationships and a new vision that will enlarge your territory and place of influence. I am taking the lid off areas of your life that have been hidden for a season. Be prepared to be out of your comfort zone.

27th June
Isaiah 66: 8
Can a country be born in a day?

It is hard to give birth on your own. Midwives play an important part in the birth process. Recognise the people around you that I have provided to assist you in birthing your dreams and visions.

28th June
Isaiah 30: 21
Your ears will hear a voice behind you, saying, 'This is the way walk in it.'

I am guiding you in answer to your prayers for the way forward. As you contemplate which decision to make I will make it clear; this is the way go forward with confidence.

29th June
Isaiah 40: 31
Those who hope in the Lord will renew their strength.

No matter how overwhelming your burdens appear; I can turn them into blessings if you will wait upon me and refuse to run.

30th June
Matthew 4: 17
Jesus began to preach, 'Repent for the Kingdom of Heaven is near.'

I have empowered you for change. Your destiny is in your hands.

July

1st July
Acts 27: 29
Fearing that we would be dashed against the rocks, they dropped four anchors from the stern and prayed for daylight.

Are you in the midst of a storm? Then there is one thing you must do. You must drop your anchors and hold fast to the word of God. If you trust my word over the storm, you will not be shipwrecked, I will come to you.

2nd July
Jonah 2: 3
You hurled me into the deep, into the very heart of the seas.

If you are in the middle of a storm because of disobedience, do not start bargaining with me. Simply thank me that I have kept you for my purpose and trust me for your deliverance.

3rd July
Acts 27: 44
The rest were to get there on planks or on pieces of the ship.

You can survive a shipwreck even if all you have left is a piece of driftwood to get you to shore. It is never over until God says it's over.

4th July
1Timothy 1: 19
Holding onto faith and a good conscience. Some have rejected these and so have shipwrecked their faith.

How do you avoid being shipwrecked in your own life, church or family? By holding onto the word of God and being sensitive to obey the small promptings of the Holy Spirit. Every step of obedience stops your heart from hardening and becoming shipwrecked.

5th July
Revelation 3: 8
See, I have placed before you an open door that no one can shut.

Are you wondering which way to go, which direction to take? Ask me to close every door that is not for you at this time and to open the one that you are to go through. Then trust me to lead you and stop worrying.

6th July
Proverbs 11: 3
The unfaithful are destroyed by their duplicity.

Beware of duplicity. Duplicity of vision and purpose will destroy you. A train that keeps changing tracks causes confusion to its' passengers. Make a decision and go with it.

7th July
Isaiah 54: 4
Do not be afraid, you will not suffer shame. Do not fear disgrace; you will not be humiliated.

Do not fear shame or humiliation when you have decided to step out and obey me, I have you covered; even your mistakes.

8th July
Habakkuk 3: 17-18
Though the fig tree does not bud, yet I will rejoice in the Lord.

Are the promises of God showing no fruit? Are you tempted to give up? Keep praising me through the barrenness of unanswered prayers and you will be amazed at the heights it will take you to. I always keep my promises.

9th July
Habakkuk 3: 17-18
I will be joyful in God my saviour.

It's never over until I say it's over. Keep praising!

10th July
1 Samuel 17: 10-11
The Philistine said, 'This day I defy the ranks of Israel.'

What is intimidating you today? Do not stand still in fear but keep going with what I have asked you to do

11th July
1 Samuel 17: 50
So David triumphed over the Philistine with a sling and a stone.

David was armed with five stones but he only needed one. What promise has God given you today? One word from God is enough to come against the giant resisting you today.

12th July
1 Samuel 17: 37
Saul replied, 'You are not able to go out against this Philistine.' David said, 'The Lord who delivered me from the paw of the lion will deliver me from the hand of this Philistine.'

There is a David and Saul in all of us. Which spirit will you walk in today, faith or fear?

13th July
2 Samuel 5: 3
They anointed David King over Israel.

Get ready for Coronation day
When you make Jesus king in your life you will know what it is to walk in your kingly anointing and authority. Do I have reign over every part of your life or are you divided in your loyalty to me. Make me king today.

14th July
Proverbs 27: 2
Let another praise you and not your own mouth.

I am eager to promote you before others; so stop doing my job for me.

15th July
1 John 4: 18
Perfect love drives out fear.

Intimidation comes through an unhealthy self-love. My love will cast out any spirit of intimidation seeking to resist you.

16th July
Proverbs 24: 10
If you falter in times of trouble, how small is your strength.

Do not let the troubles of today cause you to lose heart and faint. It is in the midst of trouble that you show your true colours. There is more strength and tenacity in you than you realise.

17th July
Nehemiah 4: 4
Hear us, O our God, for we are despised.

If the enemy cannot intimidate you one way, he will try another. It's all lies. If mocking and despising you does not hinder you, he will say you are doing something wrong. If I have told you to do something, just keep going and do not, do not, shrink back.

18th July
Genesis 8: 12
This time the dove did not return to him.

The dove has been released and there are signs of dry land again. I know you have been contained for a season but the storm is over and you are coming out.

19th July
Proverbs 11:25
A generous man will prosper.

Are you anxious for your children? Reach out to someone else's child and bless them. Sponsor a child, baby-sit, work in the Sunday school or pray for someone else's child. In watering others your own children will be blessed.

21st July
1 Samuel 3:12
I told Eli that I would judge his family for ever because of the sin he knew about.

Remember to train, nurture and discipline your child while you have time. I will judge those who relinquish their responsibility and the authority I have given them for their children. Lovingly correct and challenge when necessary, your children need their boundaries clarified.

22nd July
Isaiah 53: 4
Surely He took up our infirmities.

Are you afflicted or sick? Pray for healing for those who are in pain or suffering. As you sow into others, a harvest of healing will return to you.

23rd July
John 4: 34-36
Do not say, 'Four months more and then the harvest.'

Take every opportunity to share the gospel with someone today. Do not miss out on your harvest, both now and for eternity.

24th July
Numbers 23:18-24
God is not a man that He should lie.

Will God keep His promise to me? Yes, I am with you and will perform all that I have promised concerning you. All I ask is for your obedience. I am not a man that lies or changes His mind. I am faithful to my promises.

25th July
Proverbs 18: 20
With the harvest from his lips he is satisfied.

Speak out the promises of God over yourself. Water the seeds that are inside you. Give life to your future by speaking the word of God. You shall eat the fruit of your words.

26th July
John 8: 29
For I always do what pleases Him.

I am looking for those whose heart is to please me. When you ask the Holy Spirit what pleases me, I cannot help but show you my favour.

27th July
Revelation 21: 7
He who overcomes will inherit all this, and I will be his God and he will be my son.

Thank you for resisting the temptation you faced today. I appreciate the fact that you had made the decision to overcome before the temptation happened. I am always on your side, Father.

28th July
Revelation 12:11
They overcame him.

How do you overcome the accuser?
You overcome him by the blood of the lamb, the word of your testimony and not loving your life even unto death. Infallible.

29th July
Matthew 25: 23
You have been faithful with a few things; I will put you in charge of many things.

What are you investing your talent in today? I am looking for increase on what I have entrusted you with. Think about it: I have given you time, resources, food, money and love for you to sow in this life, to reap in the life to come.

30th July
Matthew 14: 8
She did what she could.

I am not asking for you to give what you do not have, but to give what has been given to you. I want to call you the 'good and faithful servant' when we meet.

31ˢᵗ July

I Love You, I Love You, I Love, I Love You. Just thought you needed reminding.

August

1st August
Deuteronomy 1: 21
Do not be afraid; do not be discouraged.

I know that you have tried before but this time will be different. Trust me and move past failure and discouragement into blessing.

2nd August
Isaiah 57:18 & Exodus 15:26
I have seen his ways, but I will heal him.

I am the Lord who heals you.

3rd August
Galatians 5: 16
Live by the Spirit and you will not gratify the desires of the sinful nature.

You know it is the fruit of the Holy Spirit, so why are you trying to produce these qualities yourself. You will never bear this kind of fruit without me. Ask me and I will give you the Holy Spirit and He will produce in you love for those who annoy you and self control for yourself.

4th August
Matthew 4: 19
I will make you fishers of men

Remember the boat you are sailing in is a fishing boat and not a pleasure yacht.
I am expecting you to catch fish (men) as you go on your journey in life.

5th August
2 Kings 2: 11
Suddenly a chariot of fire and horses of fire appeared and separated the two of them.

Walking in your destiny will require separation. What are you fearful of letting go of today a relationship, mentor, job or security? Whatever you are willing to be separated from for my sake will result in greater rewards later.

6th August
2 Kings 2: 9
Let me inherit a double portion of your spirit. He picked up the cloak that had fallen from Elijah.

To receive a double portion anointing you must be willing to pick up a heavier mantle of responsibility and wear it. Elijah's mantle was heavy and coarse; Elisha had to make a choice whether to pick it up or not. It did not simply fall on him. I am asking you to be willing to carry the weight of responsibility for your calling and destiny.

7th August
Jeremiah 40: 4
Look the whole country lies before you; go wherever you please.

Stop asking me for a sign and make a decision. Whatever you choose to do in this situation I will bless. Sometimes in life there is not a right or wrong road, you simply have to make a choice and step out.

8th August
Jeremiah 4: 3
Break up your fallow ground.

There are areas in your life that need breaking up and preparing for sowing. I want you to be fruitful and prosperous in every area of your life, therefore, begin today. Start work on the unproductive areas in your life such as; work, family, prayer, bible study, discipline, self-control, loving others etc.

9th August
Samuel 2: 1
David asked, 'Where shall I go?' To Hebron the Lord answered.

Hebron represents a beginning; do not underestimate the Hebron places in your life. Do not despise the opportunity before you; it will lead to greater things if you are faithful. This beginning is leading to your destiny.

10th August
Habakkuk 2: 2
Write down the revelation and make it plain.

When did you last take time to write down the future you want to see and speak it over yourself? Start proclaiming your future today by writing out your vision.

11th August
Job 22: 27-28
What you decide on will be done.

Prophesy over yourself by writing a decree according to my word. Speak it over yourself often and write one for your family, your unsaved friends and your work. See the fruit of the words you have written and spoken become established.

12th August
Hebrews 11: 6
Without faith it is impossible to please me

I am always pleased when you believe my word.

13th August
Proverbs 16: 3
Commit to the Lord whatever you do, and your plans will succeed.

Once your plans are committed to me I will establish them, then you will see them succeed.

14th August
Nehemiah 8: 10
The joy of the Lord is your strength.

Beware of self-pity. I know what you are going through and I am with you. Self-pity will open the door for the enemy to oppress you. Choose the sacrifice of praise and you will invite me into the situation.

15th August
Proverbs 31: 10
She is worth far more than rubies

Do not devalue yourself by allowing inferiority or self-consciousness to be a part of you. You are worth more than rubies to me, be confident in who you are in me. When you are in intimidating company remember how much you are worth and stand tall.

16th August
2 Corinthians 10: 12
We do not dare to compare ourselves.

It is foolish to compare yourself to others. You will either feel proud or undervalued.
I am your only standard. If you are to boast, boast only in me.

17th August
2 Corinthians 10: 17
Let him who boasts boast in the Lord.

Boasting in anything but me will always bring disappointment. Family, money, church or friends can all fail you, but I never will. Boast in me all you desire.

18th August
Luke 15: 31
My son you are always with me and everything I have is yours.

Are you angry with me because I blessed someone you thought did not deserve it? Or maybe you believe you deserve more than other people. Do not worry my child, I have seen your faithfulness and I never withhold anything from those who walk uprightly.

19th August
Proverbs 2:11
Discretion will protect you.

As you spend time in my word I will train you in the use of discernment and discretion.
Many have fallen because they have not developed these areas of discipline. Discernment is a mark of maturity and maturity comes through the knowledge of my word.

20th August
Isaiah 49: 19-21
This place is too small for us; give us more space to live in.

Do not be discouraged, keep trusting and you will see the increase. Do not be tempted to plan smaller, but keep the vision bigger than you so only I can fulfill it.

21st August
Luke 10: 19
I have given you authority to overcome all the power of the enemy; nothing will harm you.

Remember I have given you authority over all evil, do not fear

22nd August
John 10: 10
I have come that they may have life, and have it to the full.

I am God of the much more. Much more joy, much more mercy, much more love. We need to get into the overflow of my much more. Do not be content with where you are for I have much more for you.

23rd August
Proverbs 10: 22
The blessing of the Lord makes brings wealth and He adds no trouble to it.

The only way into my blessing is in my presence. The more time you spend in my presence the more you will understand the release of my blessing upon your life. There is an ocean of blessing as yet untapped because it takes time to wait in my presence.

24th August
Proverbs 21: 5
The plans of the diligent lead to profit.

Have you made any plans lately? Have you planned for this coming year? Do not wander aimlessly through another year; have a plan and submit it to me. I will orchestrate the details of your life to bring about your desires.

25th August
James 1: 7
A double minded man is unstable in all he does.

Stop weighing up every decision you make and going back on commitments. Make a decision and go with it. To keep weighing up your decisions will open the door to confusion and discouragement.

26th August
Psalm 81: 10
Open wide your mouth and I will fill it.

When was the last time you shared your testimony with anyone? You have a powerful tool at your disposal; share it with someone today.

27th August
Genesis 1 Psalm 51
In the beginning God created the heavens and the earth.

Do you want a fresh start or a new beginning? I spoke and brought order out of chaos. I can bring order out of the chaos of your life. I gave King David a fresh start after his act of murder and adultery. All he did was make a fresh commitment to change and trust me for his future.

28th August
Revelation 21: 5
I am making everything new!

I am committed to giving you a fresh start but I need your cooperation. Do the next thing you can to initiate the change you want to see. Start with a simple thing, clean the house, decorate a room, start tithing, finish what you have began and trust me for the change.

29th August
Psalm 50: 23
He who sacrifices thank-offerings honours me, and he prepares the way so that I may show him the salvation of God.

Whenever you choose to praise me in a difficult time you make a way for me to act on your behalf. I reward the sacrifices of thanksgiving, it ushers you into my very throne room. It is there you find the answers to your prayers.

30th August
1 John 1: 9
If we confess our sins, he is faithful and just and will forgive us our sins.

You are forgiven the moment you confess your sins and repent. A fresh start was written over the cross for all who would believe and receive it. The blood of my Son the Lord Jesus Christ has cleansed you from all sin. Leave the sin of yesterday, last year, the last ten, twenty years behind and move on from this day.

31st August
Psalm 118: 5-6
The Lord is with me, I will not be afraid.

Come to the word and I will strengthen and encourage you.

September

1st September
Psalm 144: 2
He is my stronghold and my deliverer.

I am your deliverer. Do you need deliverance today from fears, worries, debt, your enemies or yourself? The Spirit of the Lord God is upon you to deliver you from your enemies.

2nd September
Psalm 34: 17
He delivers them from all their troubles.

I hear your cry for help and will deliver you from all your troubles, not some, not most, but all. All I ask is that you believe on me in the heat of the trial and I will rescue you.

3rd September
Psalm 78: 9
The men of Ephraim, though armed with bows turned back on the day of battle.

There is no honour if you turn back in this battle. I am with you, your loyal King and victor. I will not leave you. You have all the armor and weapons you need to overcome. You have my Name, the covering of my Blood and the Word in your mouth.

4th September
2 Corinthians 12: 9
My power is made perfect in weakness.

I am aware of the problems you are having with work and I am with you. I will bring you through as you continue to submit the situation to me and do what is right.

5th September
Psalm 119: 32
You have set my heart free.

Do you want a heart that is free from every weight and burden? Simply choose to obey my word and leave the past with all it's cares and mistakes and run with me afresh. Do not hold on to yesterday, it will hold you back from tomorrow.

6th September
Hebrews 13: 5
Keep your lives free from the love of money.

Learn to be satisfied with me, money in itself will never satisfy you. When is enough ever enough? I will never, never fail you or leave you in your time of need. Trust me for the money you need both now and in the future.

7th September
Deut 30: 19
I have set before you life and death, blessings and curses. Now choose life.

What legacy are you going to leave behind you for those who come after you?
There is no doubt that you will leave a legacy; but how you choose to spend this day will determine what kind of legacy you will leave behind. Good or bad, blessings or curses, the choice is yours. How obedient you will you be to my word today?

8th September
Mark 16: 4
They saw the stone, that was very large, had been rolled away.

The unbelief that has kept you from my promises is being rolled away from your life today. I will bring you into a revelation of faith for all I have promised you. A stone was all that kept my disciples from knowing the power of my Promises to them.

9th September
Ezekiel 18: 19
The son who has been careful to keep all my decrees, he will surely live.

Let go of the past; stop blaming others or yourself, forgive and move on. There can be no more excuses for your life. You are the captain of your own ship and the only one responsible for where it is going. When you take responsibility for your own life and stop the blame shifting you will experience freedom and healing.

10th September
II Kings 2: 13
He picked up the cloak that had fallen from Elijah.

I am waiting to give you the double portion of My Spirit but first you must receive it. Whatever you can see with your mind and spirit by faith, you can have.

11th September
Jeremiah 29: 11
I know the plans I have for you plans to prosper you.

Will you choose to believe me when everything looks contrary to what you are praying and hoping for? When it looks like I do not know or do not care about your situation. Please believe me, my plans are to bless you, prosper you and give you a good future.

12th September
Luke 9: 51
Jesus resolutely set out for Jerusalem.

Just as Jesus set His face towards Jerusalem, make up your mind, make a commitment and keep to it. This is the only way to accomplish anything and overcome double-mindedness.

13th September
Mark 11: 5
When you stand praying, if you hold anything against anyone, forgive him.

When you bless others make sure to bless your enemies. Speak out a blessing over your enemies. Blessing them will ensure that blessings continue to flow to you and them.

14th September
Isaiah 43: 1-4
Fear not for I have redeemed you.

I am your deliverer. When the enemy comes in like a flood I will raise up a standard against him. When you go through deep rivers of trouble, whether financial, emotional or relational you will not drown, for I am with you.

15th September
Exodus 16: 21
Each morning everyone gathered as much as he needed.

I want you to have fresh manna every day. Not stale or moldy bread. I want you to come to me afresh for the living bread of my presence and word. Let my word taste good again as you come back into fellowship with me.

16th September
Isaiah 42: 1-4
A bruised reed He will not break.

I know the outburst you have recently manifested has been born out of a bruised spirit. You have allowed the fire of My Holy Spirit to dim within you and the enemy took advantage with discouragement and hurt. Come back to me and I will restore you because I delight in you.

17th September
John 10: 10
I have come that they may have life and have it to the full.

Who said you can't have it all? It was not my words. I said, 'Fear not because it pleases the Father to give you the Kingdom'. Not simply a part of the Kingdom but the whole Kingdom. Think bigger and do not settle for less than what is in your heart.

18th September
Romans 8: 28
We know that in all things, God works for the good of those who love Him.

The situations in your life that appear out of control are actually working for your good. Trust me, I am working behind the scenes of your life. Although not every thing is good in your life right now, I am nevertheless working all things for good for you. Only trust me.

19th September
Psalm 30: 11
You turned my wailing into dancing.

I am with you as much on your bad days as I am on your good and anointed days. It will not always be like this. I will turn your mourning into dancing again. I will put off your sackcloth. Though you cannot see the answer to your prayer keep praising me and I will open the way for you.

20th September
Mark 11: 22
Have faith in God.

Is there a mountain confronting you? Speak my word to the mountain and see it become a plain. Nothing is impossible to him who believes. Mountains of addiction, sickness, impossibilities will have to move as you stand on my word.

21ˢᵗ September
Numbers 20: 8
Speak to the rock before their eyes and it will pour out its water.

Speak to the rock, the hard place in your life and see rivers of blessing released. As you speak the word, the rock will release blessings like rivers. There will be no lack, my word is powerful and produces life.

22ⁿᵈ September
Exodus 34: 30
When they saw Moses' face was radiant they were afraid to come near him.

You can only use my authority when you have been in my presence. Do not allow the enemy, life or hurt to keep you out of my presence.

23ʳᵈ September
Isaiah 1: 18
Though your sins are like scarlet, they shall be as white as snow.

No matter how deep the stain of your sins, I can clean you again as new. The blood of my son can act like bleach on the darkest stain of your sin.

24th September
Hebrews 10: 22
Let us draw near to God with a sincere heart.

Come near today if you have drifted away from me; you can find your way back through the blood of my son Jesus.

25th September
Esther 5: 1
On the third day Esther put on her royal robes.

Remember who you are.
You are of royal blood, and carry royal favor and authority. Do not let people, situations or jobs intimidate you, when you walk into a room so do my angels. Walk in the dignity of who you are in me.

26th September
Exodus 14: 13
The Lord will fight for you; you need only to be still.

You will not have to fight this battle as you look to me and keep praising. I will deal with your enemies and make a way for you. I have not planned defeat for you; simply keep looking to me.

27th September
Psalm 66: 12
We went through fire and water, but you brought us to a place of abundance.

The frustration you are going through today is to test your patience, emotions and finances. But this test will bring you into a spacious place. I know you think nothing is happening but I am about to bring you into a bigger place than you ever imagined.

28th September
Galatians 6: 9
Let us not become weary in doing good.

I know that looking at circumstances can bring discouragement. I know you have tried to be faithful and obedient to me. I want to assure you that there will be a reward for not giving up in the face of discouragement. Those who have achieved greatness have kept going in the face of discouragement.

29th September
Matthew 11: 28-30
Come to me all you who are weary and burdened.

I have seen the despair in your heart and I want you to know that the heavy load you are working under is not from me. I give only light burdens. Bring your burdens to me and let me give you the rest you so greatly need. You will be surprised at the way things turn out for you in the days to come.

30th September
Proverbs 31: 25
She can laugh at the days to come.

Why does the wise woman of proverbs laugh at the days ahead of her? Because she knows from experience that the trials she is going through with her spouse, children, finances and work will end in victory as she continues to trust me and my promises to her.

October

1st October
Matthew 25: 28
For everyone who has will be given more, and he will have an abundance.

Are you using every talent I have given you for my Kingdom while there is time? If you have buried the talent I gave you, this is your day to uncover it and use it. There may not be another chance. It is not about age or qualification but about obedience and investment. Invest your talent now before it is too late.

2nd October
Psalm 37: 4
Delight yourself in the Lord and He will give you the desires of your heart.

I know how frustrated you feel waiting for the answers to your prayers. I want to give you the things you desire but I am waiting for you to want me more than the answers. Can I be your joy today, just me, with no strings attached?

3rd October

Matthew 11: 28
Come to me and you shall find rest for your souls.

The rest you are seeking is in me. It is a lie that you must carry these heavy burdens. I want you to be free of worry. As you learn more of me, your burdens will become lighter and you will learn to walk in my rest.

4th October
It is not the waiting that is hard it is how you wait!

5th October
Joel 2: 25
I will repay you for the years the locusts have eaten.

Staying angry with me will only delay the restoration you are seeking. I want to make up for lost time, lost dreams, lost hopes, lost finances and lost health. As you humble yourself and cooperate with me I will restore the years that the locust has eaten. This is my promise.

6th October
Isaiah 61: 3
To bestow on them a crown of beauty, instead of ashes.

What can you do with ashes? I can do more with a few ashes than man can with a whole gold mine. When nothing is left in your life but a few dry ashes, I can turn them into something beautiful in your life and give you a crown of authority and beauty. Never limit what I can do with the ashes left in your life.

7th October
Psalm 113: 7
He raises the poor from the dust and lifts the needy from the ash heap.

You may feel today that you are sitting on an ash heap; nothing left but loss and disappointment in your life. But I can raise you up from this place to sit with the nobles of my people. It is not over until I say it's over. I raise one up and I bring another low. Wait upon me, for nothing is too difficult for me and your future is secure in my hands.

8th October
Psalm 92:10
You have exalted my horn like that of a wild ox.

I will give strength to those who wait upon me and I will increase strength, honour and dignity. Your anointing will be like that of a wild ox and nothing shall make you afraid.

9th October
Psalm 112: 3
Wealth and riches are in his house.

When a man fears me he will find blessing, prosperity and wealth in his house. I do not plan for my children to live in lack; I am the all-sufficient God. I am the God of more than enough.

10th October
1 Thessalonians 5: 18
Give thanks in all circumstances.

Attitude determines your altitude. Do you desire to come up higher today? Then start thanking me for all the blessings you have in your life. Find a reason to praise me in your lowest moments and you will walk in a fresh anointing in the Spirit.

11th October
Mark 11: 22
Have faith in God.

Go all the way. Mediocrity belongs to those who only go halfway up the mountain. But this is not you. I am calling you to go all the way. Do not give up because there is still a mountain to take; the summit is in view and you can do it. Not by might or by power but by My Spirit says the Lord.

12th October
Matthew 1: 21
She will give birth to a son.

Keep bearing down. I will give you strength to bear, to bring forth. Keep pushing until you birth your vision. The resistance you are facing is birth pain. Keep pushing.

13th October
James 3: 16
For where you have envy, there you will find disorder and every evil practice.

Do not take the bait of jealousy. Do not get jealous of someone else's success or promotion. I have not forgotten you. Do not keep looking at others but keep focused on me.

14th October
Numbers 11: 1
Now the people complained about their hardships in the hearing of the Lord.

Complaining only robs you of anointing. Be grateful for your life and all that I have planned for you. See your menial tasks as important in my sight and they will give you more fulfillment. Do your tasks with an excellent spirit and not simply grudgingly.

15th October
Hebrews 4: 16
Let us then approach the throne of grace with confidence.

You do not have to fear coming into my presence. I am always ready to receive you. Before you enter my presence in the throne room, your name is being called, announcing your arrival. Heaven understands the excitement I have when you draw near to me.

16th October
Hebrews 10: 19,22
Since we have confidence to enter the Most Holy Place.

Come near, even if you have not graced my presence for a while. The blood of my Son covers you; there is no need to feel ashamed. Simply come, I am waiting to sit with you and have time with you again.

17th October
Romans 8: 26
The Spirit helps us in our weakness.

Are you worried, needing guidance? Remember you can ask the Holy Spirit to help you. Pray in your heavenly prayer language and I will understand your heart. I will fill your thoughts with my thoughts, trust me.

18th October
Habakkuk 2: 2
Write down the revelation and make it plain on tablets.

Once you have written down your vision and the promises I have made to you. This will keep the vision alive in you. I never forget a promise I have made and will bring it about at the appointed time.

19th October
Joshua 6: 14
As commander of the army of the Lord I have now come.

I am not coming to bless your next venture; I am coming to take over. I do not want what is left over from a busy life. I want all of you and that will mean being obedience to all I ask. If you give me all of you, I promise to do more with your life than you could possibly ask or imagine.

20th October
Mark 4: 30
What shall we say the Kingdom of God is like?

Do not despise the small things in your life. My Kingdom comes as a small mustard seed that grows into the largest tree in the garden. Do not judge things as they are at this time. All you are waiting for is contained within a tiny seed. Where is that tiny seed planted? It is within you.

21ˢᵗ October
Psalm 23
The Lord is my Shepherd; I shall not be in want
Goodness and love will follow me
He guides me in paths of righteousness for His name's sake
You anoint my head with oil.

22ⁿᵈ October
Isaiah 41: 10
Do not fear, for I am with you; do not be dismayed, for I am your God. I will strengthen you and help you. I will uphold you with my righteous right hand.

Do not fear what is confronting you right now. The enemy wants you to believe that there is no way out and you will be put to shame. I am faithful and will bring you through this attack victoriously if you continue to trust me.

23ʳᵈ October
Isaiah 49: 24
Can plunder be taken from warriors, or captives rescued from the fierce?

Are there members of your friends or family that seem to be held captive from the truth? Do not fear. I am mightier than their oppressors. I will contend with their enemies and rescue your children. I am your redeemer, your Saviour and the Mighty one of Jacob.

24th October
Judges 6: 12
The Lord is with you, mighty man of fearless courage.

You are mighty in my eyes. See yourself as I see you. I see you as one called to lead many. Do not allow your self to be put down in any way. Believe in yourself as I believe in you.

25th October
Judges 6: 34
Then the spirit of the Lord came upon Gideon, and he blew a trumpet summoning the Abiezrites to follow him.

I will equip you with everything you need to lead. I will clothe you with myself and others will be drawn to you because of me. My favour will be seen upon you.

26th October
Isaiah 41: 13
Do not fear; I will help you.

I have called you as a leader and as a leader you must deal with any fear in your life. All fear of rejection; shame, failure, man, criticism, change, being out of control or making mistakes, must die. Fear will not only stunt your growth but also those you are called to lead.

27th October
Matthew 6: 25
I tell you, do not worry about your life.

Do not worry about what you are to eat or drink; I have provided for all your needs. Keep focused on me and refuse to worry about the needs you have.
Living one day at a time keeps you from being consumed with worry about the future.

28th October
Exodus 20: 12
Honour your father and your mother.

When was the last time you contacted your parents and thanked them or told them you loved them?
You are never too old to honour your parents by respecting and loving them.

29th October
Judges 6: 12
The Lord is with you mighty warrior.

I am not looking at your weaknesses and failures. I am looking at the greatness I see in you. I am getting ready to release you and use for my glory. I do not think like you or see as you see; you may have to exchange your focus.

30th October
Judges 6: 11
Gideon was threshing wheat in a winepress to keep it from the Midianites.

Circumstances have made you want to hide. However comfortable that may feel; it is time to come out of hiding and be who you were called to be. I have called you to leadership and your obedience will be the key that unlocks the circumstances you find yourself in.

31st October
1 Samuel 8: 1-3
But his sons did not walk in his ways

If your grown children are demanding independence and do not want to follow me; understand, you can no longer control them. Stop blaming yourself for your mistakes and missed opportunities and hand them over to me. I am faithful and I have not finished with them yet. Keep praying for them.

November

1st November
Genesis 12: 10
Now there was a famine in the land and Abraham went down to Egypt to live there.

Abraham experienced a time of famine when he stepped out in obedience to me. In times of testing it is important to hold onto my word and promise and keep moving forward. Your famine will turn into abundance if you keep in obedience and do not give up.

2nd November
1 Peter 1: 15
Be Holy, because I am Holy.

I am asking you to be holy, not to do holy. Holiness will take you to places even the anointing will not. You can minister like me with the anointing but you need holiness to be like me.

3rd November
Exodus 2: 9
Take this baby and nurse him for me and I will pay you.

Whatever I ask you to take on for me will come with the resources and funds you need.
I will provide for you as you fulfill my call upon your life. I will send people with the finances to assist you. Do not worry where the provision will come from when you are fulfilling your dream.

4th November
Matthew 6: 10
If he asks for a fish, will you give him a snake?

Trust me that the relationship, job, child, spouse that has come in answer to your prayer is for your blessing and not to harm you. Trust me as you speak the word over your situation, it will turn around for your good.

5th November
Psalm 42: 5
Why are you downcast, O my soul?

Why are you depressed over that situation, trust in me and you shall yet praise me. I want you to trust me in times of trouble so that I can rescue you and you will glorify me.

6th November
Psalm 101: 2
I will walk in my house with blameless heart.

Integrity is what you are in private when no one is around. Always live for the audience of one, me. Do not compromise what is right because no one can see you. Walk blameless in the privacy of your own home.

7th November
Psalm 101: 5
Whoever slanders his neighbour in secret, him will I put to silence.

When you speak of others even in private, consider I hear every word. You will be accountable for your words in eternity.

8th November
Ruth 1:16
Where you go I will go.

Your relationships will determine where your destiny will go. There will always be people who will leave you and those who will share life with you. No one can fulfill his or her destiny alone. The relationships I give you are essential for bringing about my purposes.

9th November
1 Kings 19: 20
Elisha then left his oxen and ran after Elijah.

Elisha was willing to leave his family and livelihood to follow my prophet and his own destiny. Elisha served Elijah faithfully for twenty years before he was released into his own ministry. Be faithful where I call you and I will release you in my time.
Align yourself with my anointed ministries that will prepare you for future service.

10th November
Luke 18:1
Jesus told his disciples that they should always pray and not give up.

Prayer changes things!
Pray Today!

11th November
Luke 6: 12
Jesus went out to a mountainside to pray, and spent the night praying to God.

Keep praying and do not give up. Be persistent until you see your answer.

12th November
Psalm 5: 3
In the morning, O Lord, you hear my voice; in the morning, I lay my requests before you and wait in expectation.

There is no better time than the morning to meet me. You will be more prepared to face the challenges of the day when you have been in my presence at the start of the day.

13th November
Proverbs 4: 7
Wisdom is supreme; therefore get wisdom.

The benefits of wisdom: long life, promotion, prosperity, success, health, protection, riches, honour and peace. Ask me for wisdom today. Jesus is your wisdom; seek Him.

14th November
Matthew 6: 9
Our Father in Heaven hallowed be your name.

May the name of Jesus be lifted up and honoured in your life, home family, work and church.

15th November
Matthew 6: 10
Your Kingdom come your will be done.

My Kingdom is righteousness, peace and joy in the Holy Spirit.

16th November
Matthew 6: 11
Give us today our daily bread.

Share your needs with me today. I have promised to give you everything that pertains to life and godliness.

17th November
Matthew 6: 12
Forgive us our debts, as we also have forgiven our debtors.

Who do you need to forgive today? Release forgiveness to the person who has hurt you and let you down. This will release the forgiveness you need from me today.

18th November
Nehemiah 6: 3
They were scheming to harm me.

When opposition arises do not become reactionary, but wait before me until peace comes. Pray in your prayer language when you do not know what to pray and trust me to turn the situation around. Know how to respond in me and not simply react in the flesh.

19th November
John 13: 7
You do not realize now what I am doing, but later you will understand.

*I know you do not understand what is going on at the moment.
Do not worry, but trust me to lead you through your perplexity. One day soon you will understand that all things have turned around for your good.*

20th November
Ruth 3: 18
Wait, my daughter, until you find out what happens. For the man will not rest until the matter is settled today.

Be patient, God is at work and will not rest until He settles the matter that is on your heart. Today!

21st November
2 Corinthians 4: 17
So we fix our eyes not on what is seen, but on what is unseen.

Where is your focus? Think on those things that bring praise, joy and peace. Do not keep focused on the problem but look to me. If you keep looking at the problem you will not walk in victory.

22nd November
Jude 24
To Him who is able to keep you from falling and to present you before His glorious presence without fault and with great joy. To the only God our Saviour be glory, majesty, power and authority, through Jesus Christ our Lord, before all ages, now and for evermore! Amen

23rd November
1 Peter 2: 24
He Himself bore our sins in His body on the tree, so that we might die to sins and live for righteousness.

There is hope! You can be finished with sin and live a good life. This is reality in Christ not wishful thinking. Clothe yourself with the new nature Christ has given you.

24th November
Colossians 3: 9
You have taken off your old self with its practices and have put on the new self.

Put off, put on. What do you do with unwanted behaviour and habits? Cast off the old and put on the new you in Jesus. Do not allow sin to stay in your life. Every addiction can be broken in the name of Jesus.

25th November
Jude 23
Snatch others from the fire and save them.

Be urgent for souls. Snatch them from the very fire by your prayers and love. Lay up treasure in heaven.

26th November
1 John 2: 25
And this is what he promised us, even eternal life.

Never shift from trusting me to save you. Never believe you are too far from my help and deliverance.

27th November
Malachi 3: 3
He will purify the Levites and refine them like gold or silver.

Every test you are going through is to refine you and to bring me glory by producing gold in you. Do not settle for less than gold. Do not rebel against the tests but submit to me in them.

28th November
Isaiah 43:1-3
When you walk through the fire you will not be burned.

When you go through the fires of oppression, I have promised that you will not be destroyed.
You can come through this time of testing like Daniel's friends and not even have the smell of the fire on you.

29th November
Psalm 139: 14
I am fearfully and wonderfully made.

What you think about yourself determines the outcome of your life. Your heart and body believe what your mind tells it. Tell yourself how amazing God has made you.

30th November
1 John 2:15
If anyone loves the world, the love of the father is not in him.

Beware of the lusts that fight against your soul, the lust of the flesh, the lust of the eyes and boasting.

31st November
Galatians 5: 16
Live by the Spirit, and you will not gratify the desires of the sinful nature.

Only the power of the Holy Spirit will overcome the lusts and demands of your flesh!

December

1st December
Luke 2: 14
Glory to God in the Highest, and on earth peace to men on whom His favour rests.

My favour and peace are given to those who seek to please me. As you desire to make your plans and decisions in the light of my will, you will know peace and blessing.

2nd December
Luke 4: 19
To proclaim the year of the Lord's favour.

This is the year of the Lord's favour upon you. I delight in you and see you as you step out in obedience to me. My favour rests upon you. My favour is the grace and supernatural ability to carry out that which I have called you to.

3rd December
Luke 2: 40
The child grew and became strong; he was filled with wisdom, and the grace of God was upon him.

Expect divine favour to increase upon your life and your work. As you continue to grow in me, my favour will increase. Those around you will witness my favour and want to bless you as you move forward in your destiny.

4th December
Luke 4:19
The Spirit of the Lord is upon me to proclaim the year of the Lord's favour.

The Lord has anointed you to proclaim the year of the Lord's favour. The Holy Spirit is the one who will reveal my favour to you. As you walk in the power of the Holy Spirit you will be able to percieve and receive my favour. You will then be anointed to proclaim the day of my favour to others.

5th December
Matthew 2:12
Having been warned in a dream not to go back to Herod, they returned to their country by another route.

Dreams can be a way of warning us of coming danger. If you have a dream that concerns you then pray with someone about it or seek a leader's advice. Maybe the dream is trying to divert trouble coming to you.

6th December
Matthew 1: 20
An angel of the Lord appeared to him in a dream.

Dreams are often used to give direction or guidance. These dreams are usually clear to remember and offer specific words or pictures reflecting the way forward. Pray and ask for clear revelation regarding them.

7th December
Ephesians 4: 26
In your anger do not sin.

Check yourself to see if the anger that erupts in you is justified or if it is a manifestation of past hurt that I can heal.

8th December
Ephesians 4: 31
Get rid of all bitterness, rage and anger, brawling and slander, along with every form of malice.

Anger is a self-destructive force in your life. If you experience outbursts of anger ask me to show you where these strong emotions came into your life. Then repent, put off the anger and put on the nature of Jesus Christ.

9th December
Ephesians 4: 32
Be kind and compassionate to one another, forgiving each other, just as in Christ God forgave you.

Keep releasing forgiveness to those who cause you to feel angry and ask me for my love for them. Remember, vengeance is mine.

10th December
Matthew 2:13 and 21
So he got up, took the child and his mother during the night and left for Egypt.
So he got up, took the child and his mother and went to the land of Israel.

Mary and Joseph had to keep moving homes because of Jesus. They were being obedient to my leading and fulfilling prophecy. Do not be intimidated by any move I ask you to make. My plan is perfect and I promise to take care of you wherever you go.

11th December
Luke 2: 6
The time came for the baby to be born.

Birthing is a messing business; when you are ready to birth your dream or vision get alone with me. Birth is a private not a public event. I want to be the one at your side giving you the strength to bear and not abort your dream.

12th December
Luke 2: 7
She gave birth to her firstborn, a son.

Birth is a painful experience. Pushing the baby out is hard and painful and you think you may die in the process. See beyond the pain of birthing, to the baby being born.
You cannot run away in the middle of birthing a baby! You have to stay and see it through. Do not abandon your dream because of the pain!

13th December
Romans 5: 19
Through the obedience of the one man the many will be made righteous.

One man can make a difference! Sin came in through one man, Adam. Righteousness came from one man, Jesus!

14th December
Romans 5: 20
Where sin increased, grace increased all the more.

Through Adam sin, death and judgment came into the world.
But through Jesus Christ came righteousness, life and grace
Because grace came in such a greater measure than sin we can know freedom, healing and life in abundance.

5th December
Ezekiel 3: 16
At the end of seven days the word of the Lord came to me.

Ezekiel sat quiet in his house for seven days. At the end of seven days God spoke to him. How about taking some time out in this busy season to seek God, He may be waiting to speak to you.

16th December
Mark 16: 15
Go into all the world and preach the good news to all creation.

Go where? Everywhere! Do what? Preach the gospel! To who? Everyone! This is not an option it is a command.

17th December
Matthew 28: 16
Baptise them in the name of the Father and of the Son and of the Holy Spirit, and teach them to obey everything I have commanded you.

What are Jesus' commands? Repent and be baptized. Love one another and be filled with the Holy Spirit. Who have you shared your faith with recently?

18th December
Deuteronomy 10: 17
For the Lord your God is God of Gods and Lord of Lords, the Great God, mighty and awesome.

I am the Great God and my seed of greatness is in you. I want you to walk in Greatness and not settle for good or even the best life, but a Great life. Speak greatness over yourself today, great health, great relationships, great marriage, great children. Do not settle for I am the Great God.

19th December
Genesis 8: 20
Then Noah built an altar to the Lord.

When the storm had passed and transition was over the first thing Noah did was to build an altar to me. Before he moved on and built a house, started a business or made plans for the future he built an altar to me. If you are waiting to go into the next season of your life, build an altar. Put me first and I will lead you.

20th December
Genesis 8: 20
Then Noah built an altar to the Lord.

After the flood Noah built an altar to the Lord. After he had lost everything but his family and some animals. After he had lost the house, the car, relations, friends, neighbours and livelihood, then he built an altar. What did he put on the altar? Ashes: he knew that I would give him beauty for the ashes that were left of his life.

21st December
Philippians 4: 6
Do not be anxious about anything!

Do not worry. Worry is a thief that robs you of peace, health, wealth, life and youthfulness. Today give your burdens to me and move on in the knowledge that I will take care of your problems and deliver you from the thief, who comes to steal, kill and destroy you.

22nd December
Psalm 61: 2
I call as my heart grows faint, lead me to the rock that is higher than I.

When the pressures of life overwhelm you there is a place to go. Jesus is the rock that will hold you when times are so challenging you can hardly breathe. He is the one to run to. Stand against the spirit that overwhelms you in the mighty name of Jesus and command it to back off!

23rd December
1 Corinthians 16: 9
A great door for effective work has opened to me, and there are many that oppose me.

I have not just opened a door for you but a 'great' door. There may be many that oppose the destiny I have for you but they cannot shut you out of your destiny. I have opened a door for you that no man can shut and it is a great work!

24th December
Ecclesiastes 9: 7
Eat your food with gladness and drink your wine with a joyful heart, for it is now that God favours what you do.

I want you to enjoy life and not simply endure it. My favour is on you today so do not wait for the perfect circumstances to enjoy what I have given you. Enjoy your wife, your husband, your children and your life.

25th December
Ecclesiastes 11: 4
Whoever watches the wind will not plant; whoever looks at the clouds will not reap.

Do not wait for the perfect time, the perfect church, or the perfect person before you step out and act. Life does not always offer perfect solutions and perfect opportunities and faith in me will require taking risks. Seize the moment and take life with both hands.

26th December
Job 42: 12
The Lord blessed the latter part of Job's life more than the first.

My desire is always to bless you and for you to increase more and more you and your family. Whatever heartache you have suffered in the past, I want you to know that my plan is still to bless you. Your latter years will be greater than the past.

27ᵗʰ December
Revelation 21: 4
He will wipe every tear from their eyes.

Weeping may endure for a season but joy comes in the morning. I am going to make all things new and your tears will be forgotten for the joy of being in my presence. I am the Alpha and the Omega the beginning and the end of all things. I was at your beginning and I will be at your end. Do not fear.

28ᵗʰ December
Psalm 130: 7
Put your hope in the Lord, for with the Lord is unfailing love and with Him is full redemption.

At the end of another year I want you to continue to hope in me, for I will never let you down or fail you. I can redeem all that you have lost this year if you will surrender it to me. I have covered this past year with my love and grace do not fear.

29ᵗʰ December
Proverbs 27: 18
He who looks after his master will be honoured.

Let everything you do bring glory to Jesus while you can and the day will come when He will be honoring you.

30th December
Psalm 90: 12
Teach us to number our days aright.

As we reflect on the past year, let us give attention to the year ahead. Keep in mind how precious one day, one week or one year can be.
Plan the coming year as though you did not have all the time in the world.

31st December
Psalm 39: 4
Show me O Lord, my life's end and the number of my days.

All of us have a certain amount of time allotted to us. Let us use them wisely and productively knowing that every moment really can count for Jesus! He is coming back soon!

Made in the USA
Charleston, SC
05 February 2013